YOU CAN'T TAKE IT WITH YOU,
SO EAT IT NOW!

**OTHER BOOKS BY
NICOLE HOLLANDER**

I'm in Training to Be Tall
and Blonde

Ma, Can I Be a Feminist and
Still Like Men?

That Woman Must Be on Drugs

Mercy, It's the Revolution and
I'm in My Bathrobe

My Weight Is Always Perfect for
My Height—Which Varies

Hi, This Is Sylvia

Sylvia on Sundays

Okay, Thinner Thighs for Everyone

Never Tell Your Mother This Dream

The Whole Enchilada

Never Take Your Cat to a Salad Bar

YOU CAN'T TAKE IT WITH YOU, SO EAT IT NOW!

Everyday Strategies from Sylvia by

Nicole Hollander

Vintage Books
A Division of Random House, Inc.
New York

A Vintage Original, May 1989
First Edition
Copyright ©1987, 1988, 1989 by Nicole Hollander

Library of Congress Cataloging-in-Publication Data
Hollander, Nicole.
   You can't take it with you so eat it now.
   "A Vintage original"—T.p. verso.
   I. Sylvia.   II. Title.
PN6728.S97H69   1989   741.5'973   88-40369
ISBN 0-679-72236-X (pbk.)

Design by Tom Greensfelder
Manufactured in the United States of America
10 9 8 7 6 5 4 3 2 1

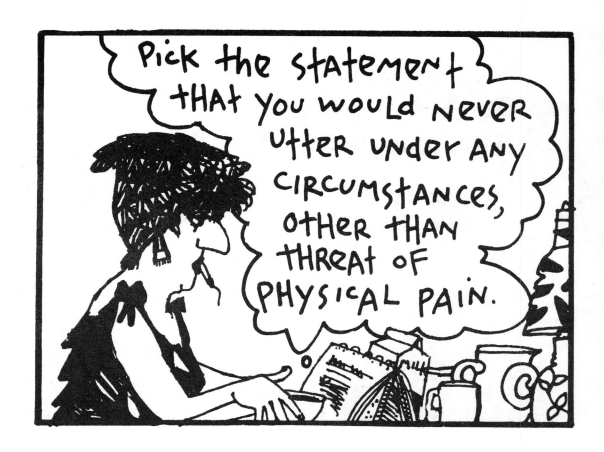

10

Some Pentagon Employees WILL **Lie** At the PEARLY Gates.

DiD YoU take bribes to steer business to certain Defense contractors?

12

I'M AFRAID I HAVE SHORT TERM MEMORY LOSS.

LET'S BE REASONABLE THERAPY

the specter of ALZHEIMER'S DISEASE MAKES ALL OF US OVERLY SENSITIVE TO NORMAL FORGETFULNESS.

So you're Sure it isn't Anything to WORRY About?

WHAT isn't?

the DEVIL ANSWERS QUESTIONS ABOUT HELL

I've GOTTEN LOTS OF LETTERS RECENTLY, ASKING "IS there 'GLASNOST' IN HELL?" Nope, there isn't.

MANY OF US FEEL the temperATURE should be Lowered.

OH REALLY? too BAD.

the DOLLAR FELL SHARPLY today, SLIGHTLY INJURING A New Yorker on His WAY to WORK. "I didn't think MUCH of it At First because there's ALWAYS STUFF

FALLING OFF buildings Here," said A bystander. "But then I noticed it WAS dollars, AND I THOUGHT I'D PICK some up. But then I THOUGHT: 'WHY BOTHER?'"

Genetic Misunder-standings.

So these scientists CHANGE A Gene on A PiG AND then they APPLY FOR A PATENT As iF they invented A New KIND OF PiG. It's APPALLING.

JEANS ON A PiG? Boy, they Must be extra, extra LArGe. PERSONALLY I'D be AFRAID to try. AND SLIP Jeans ON A PiG. IF PEOPLE WANT them dressed, I THINK SOMETHING LOOSE FITTING, LIKE A MUUMUU WOULD be better.

15

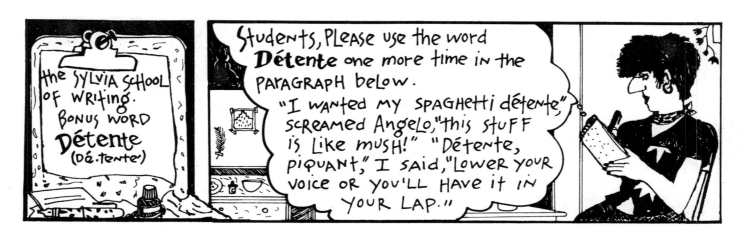

the Insurance Industry announced new regulations today requiring single men between 18 and 40 to submit proof that they have subscribed to "Penthouse" or "Hustler" for at least ten years

23

St. Lynda, Patron Saint of people who make the same mistake over and over again.

St. Lynda, martyred (pelted with uncooked rice by the assembled guests) at her wedding ceremony for saying: "OH NO, DID I JUST GET MARRIED AGAIN?"

Defensive cats...

I don't care if statistics say that cats sleep 65% of the time. You can make statistics prove anything. I WASN'T ASLEEP. I was thinking about something you said the other day. Something that hurt me deeply.

MINE

MINE AS WELL

24

the *interpretation* of DREAMS

where is CARL JUNG WHEN we NEED HiM the MOST?

I DREAMt THAT SOME insurance COMPANIES were BEING SUED by the Attorneys GENERAL OF eight States for CREATING A PHONEY insurance CRISIS, AND CONSPIRING to CREATE A boycott to REDUCE insurance AVAILABILITY IN AN EFFORT to RAISE their PROFITS, but MY THERAPIST SAID it WAS REALLY A dream About MY MOTHER.

the Rhino Series

☐1. I DON't FEAR AN I.R.S. Audit. IN FACT I'd LiKE A cHANCE to SHOW OFF MY impeccable RECORD keeping to some-one WHO COULD REALLY APPRECIATE it.

☐2. I'd RATHER FRENCH KiSS A RHINO.

Alien Love♥ - Can two people from different worlds find harmonious love even though one of them has some odd chums?

Sweetness -

— Honey.

"What do you think we should give Moammar Khadafy and his new wife for a wedding gift?" he asked me. "I didn't know you knew Moammar," I said, rather dazed. "Oh, yes," he smiled, "we grew up together." "Here?" I asked. "Well, where else," he answered, looking puzzled.

Hi, this is Sylvia's Werewolf Hotline. Does your body undergo startling changes at inopportune moments? Does "Hirsute" not even begin to describe the problem? Leave your name and number at the sound of the beep, and we'll get back to you before the full moon.

Ring! Ring!

SuperHeroes OF Public Transportation.

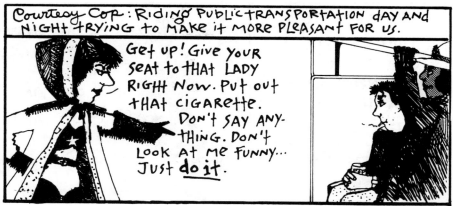

Courtesy Cop: RIDING PUBLIC TRANSPORTATION DAY AND NIGHT TRYING TO MAKE IT MORE PLEASANT FOR US.

Get up! Give your seat to THAT LADY RIGHT NOW. Put out THAT CIGARETTE. Don't SAY ANYTHING. DON'T LOOK AT ME FUNNY... Just **do it**.

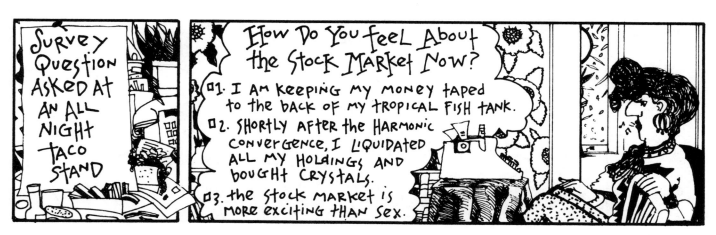

Survey Question ASKED AT AN ALL NIGHT TACO STAND

How Do You feel About the Stock MARKET Now?

☐1. I AM KEEPING MY MONEY TAPED to the BACK OF MY TROPICAL FISH TANK.

☐2. SHORTLY AFTER the HARMONIC CONVERGENCE, I LIQUIDATED ALL MY HOLDINGS AND BOUGHT CRYSTALS.

☐3. the STOCK MARKET IS MORE EXCITING THAN SEX.

How to recognize Maturity

GROWN-UPS NEVER ATTACH THEIR FAVORITE POSTERS to the WALL WITH LITTLE ROLLED UP PIECES OF SCOTCH TAPE.

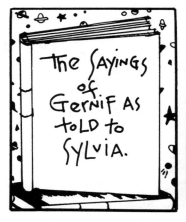

THE SAYINGS of GERNIF AS TOLD TO SYLVIA.

Brieef suit carrizs nyet fluttorbuggs.

SLOW DOWN.

"THERE ARE NO MOTHS ON A BIKINI."

IT's SO COLD, MY CAR WON'T START, AND DON'T YOU DARE SAY: "THERE ARE NO MOTHS ON A BIKINI."

I WOULDN'T DREAM OF IT.

MID-YEAR Resolutions OF the BARELY-UNDER-CONTROL

I will try to be more understanding of others. I will try to be more patient when dealing with the incompetent people that surround me. I will not SLAP anyone First thing in the MORNING.

the Buck stops before it Gets Here.

— CAREER?

I see MANY MEN LINING UP to See You.

Actress?

BANK Teller.

I'M NOT PAYING FOR this.

Actress.

Survey Question

ASKED OF A BUNCH OF KIDS UNSCREWING the top OFF A FIRE HYDRANT.

WHO WOULD YOU MOST LIKE to be STRANDED WITH ON A DESERT ISLAND?

☐ 1. the FRUGAL GOURMET.
☐ 2. JULIA CHILD.
☐ 3. SOMEONE WITH A BOAT.

Yes, I brought the FILM in to be developed in the spring OR FALL OF '79. I've been busy. UH HUH, pictures of CATS.

Alien Love CAN LOVERS from different WORLDS FIND UNDERSTANDING AND total ECSTASY ALL the time?

those ARE BAGS HONEY.

YOU HAVE Bette Davis Eyes.

I HADN'T SLEPT WELL FOR weeks WORRYING ABOUT the SITUATION in the PERSIAN GULF WHEN He CAME to ME AND ASKED, "WOULD YOU LIKE ME to try AND GET KHOMEINI AND REAGAN to TALK it OVER FACE-to-FACE? PERHAPS I COULD INVITE them to LUNCH." "SURE", I SAID IRRITABLY, "Let's invite them both FOR BARBECUED SPARE ribs." "JUST KIDDING," I SCREAMED, but he WAS ALREADY out the door.

CAT LIES OF THE RICH AND TRI-LINGUAL

OUI, I DID GIVE BEAUCOUP DINERO TO MY CHER AMI, LE COLONEL EL NORTE, AND I WOULD DO IT AGAIN, BECAUSE WE ARE BOTH MARINES.

AN INTIMATE DINNER FOR RAISA GORBACHEV, HOSTED BY NANCY REAGAN, ENDED ABRUPTLY THIS EVENING WHEN RAISA SAT ON A LEMON MERINGUE TART.

"MRS. REAGAN ASSURES US THAT SHE HAD NO IDEA RAISA WAS GOING TO SIT THERE," SAID A WHITE HOUSE SPOKESPERSON

47

51

Between Love and Madness Lies...

Obsession.

Shopping.

ARCHI-COP! Flying Hither and Yon calling Architects to task for their follies.

For tearing down beautiful old buildings to make way for hideous structures that scar our urban environment, and stand as a monument to your arrogance, I have a warrant for your arrest.

Gregor! Someone here to see you.

Tell him it's the firm down the hall.

CHATS WITH THE DEVIL

the Devil Reminisces About when he AND the Supreme being were STILL IN touch.

He was going to MAKE "Thou SHALT NOT WHINE" one of the commandments. I TALKED HIM INTO "Thou SHALT NOT covet thy NEIGHBOR'S WIFE, etc." WHICH, AT the time, I feLT WOULD CAUSE LESS trouble.

ANxiety CheckList FOR the MORNING

I don't WANT to.

☐1. IF I close my eyes brieFLY, WILL I MISS WORK?

☐2. Do I HAVE exAct CHANGE?

☐3. WILL EVERYONE ON the bus SMELL Nice?

the MILK IS "IFFY"

59

LADIES AND GENTLEMEN, WE HAVE THREE entrees this Afternoon. PLEASE SELECT ONE, but keep AN ALTERNATE IN MIND AS WE MAY RUN OUT OF your first choice. the entrees Are: Pig KNUCKLES ON A HOT CROISSANT, MENUDO AND LIVER AU GRATIN, OR eeL CHARDONNAY.

Hi. WOULD YOU MIND IF I GOT AHEAD OF YOU IN LINE?

NO, YOU CAN'T. Don't Bother Me.

500 LBS Kitty Litter

WHAT IF I SAID THAT WAITING IN LINE MAKES ME CLAUSTROPHOBIC, WOULD THAT MOVE YOU? WHAT IF I TOLD YOU I WORK FOR THE I.R.S. AND COULD AUDIT YOUR RETURN, SEIZE ALL YOUR PROPERTY, AND RUIN YOUR LIFE?

WELL, IF YOU'RE REALLY IN A HURRY...

Lives of Susan — comedy mini-series about a woman who has a 3-way split personality: housewife, waitress, and fundraiser.

Glued to the tube by her fascination with the Iran/Contra hearings, Susan neglects her home and personal appearance. When her husband suggests that she's starting to look like a Contra, Susan's anger brings forth her Oliver North persona and she tries to build an airstrip on his forehead.

Shredding parties
June 10 Martha
June 17 Edgar
June 27 to be announced

George Bush, Edwin Meese and General Noriega called a joint news conference today to say: they didn't know about it, it isn't true, and to just stop bringing it up.

WHY DO they WANT this GUY SO BADLY?

He's BIONIC.

WE ALL WANT HIM.

WATCH OUT FOR CATS WHO TRY TO PLAY ON YOUR GUILT.

CATS

WE JUST FOUND OUT WE WERE NEUTERED. WE'RE HERE TO DISCUSS HOW YOU'RE GOING TO MAKE IT UP TO US.

-Hiss!

IT WAS NOT!

BELIEVE ME FELLAHS... IT WAS ALL HER IDEA.

Like the PHARAOH'S tomb,

FULL OF MARVELOUS THINGS,

AND HAUNTED by the MUMMY'S CURSE.

WHAT HAVE YOU SAID RECENTLY THAT YOU NEVER IMAGINED YOU'D HEAR YOURSELF SAY?

#1. DO YOU CARRY ANY ULTRA-THIN LATEX CONDOMS WITH RESERVOIR TIPS, NONOXYNOL 9 SPERMICIDAL LUBRICANT, AND DECORATED WITH STARS AND CRESCENT MOONS ON A DARK BLUE BACKGROUND?

Nostalgia Quiz
Test your memory

I don't remember anything that happened before lunch.

I remember everything that ever happened. Want me to tell you?

The historic "INF" treaty was signed between the United States and the Soviet Union in 1988. Do you remember what "INF" stands for?

☐1. "Are you kidding? No one remembers that."

☐2. "Itty-Bitty Nuclear Freeze?"

Rita—do we have any lemon bars left?

I think you ate the last one in '87.

Dear U.S. Postal Service, while I'm delighted that you have issued "Cat Commemoratives", they don't quite cut it. Enclosed please find the "Sylvia Commemoratives"

USA 25 — Allergic Person and Cat — Hupchew!

USA 25 — White Cat Shedding

USA — Cat Sitting on Pizza

USA 25 — Cats Reject New Food

USA 25 — Cat Shreds Couch

USA 25

Alien Love... Can a woman from a large midwestern town find endless love on a distant planet?

MY ANGEL.

COOKIE FACE.

"MY ANGEL," he said, "I know you miss your women friends, so I invited two high-spirited gals over for tea." "WHO?" I asked, FEARFULLY. "NANCY AND RAISA," He Answered. "WHY not get MAGGIE thatcher AND MAKE MY DAY complete?" I asked, FORGETTING that Irony is Lost on the men of his planet... "WAIT!" I shouted, but He was out the door.

WHAT'S "the DISGUSTING Diet Special?"

Menu

COTTAGE CHEESE WITH CATSUP... ALL YOU CAN EAT.

ASK the CHEF About His DISGUSTING Desserts.

I think I'LL SKIP LUNCH.... SORRY, RUBY.

THAT'S OKAY. YOU HAVE TO PAY ANYWAY, OR WE MAKE YOU EAT IT.

I'd been working HARD on my "History of the hobbies of 17th Century Popes" when He called up to Me: "I'M Going out, can I bring you back something?" "Tom Cruise on toast," I said, and added, "Just kidding," but He was already out the door. "WHOOPS!" I said to myself.

72

PASTA dreams

I DREAMt THAT I WAS being chased by A HuGE drooLING Monster. I WAS trying to RUN but I kept tripping over MY SHoeLACES. I Looked down AND SAW THAT MY SHoes were LACeD WITH SPAGHetti covered WITH tiny CLAMS, pine NUtS AND A CREAM SAUce.

A SuRprise PARty FoR NANcy ReagaN, hosted by DoN ReGAN AND RAisa GoRbacHev, ENDED AbRuptLy this EVENING WHEN NANcy bit RAisA.

"the INcIDENt WAS bLown out of PRoPoRTIoN," SAID A WHite House SpokespeRson.

The Rhino Series

☐1. I would welcome the opportunity to defend the validity of Shere Hite's methodology with a roomful of men.

☐2. I'd rather have a rhino tap dance on my noggin.

MA, WHEN Are you coming out?

Honey, use the other bathroom.

MA, we don't have another bathroom.

the one with the skylight, and the built-in sauna...

I hate this.

to the left of the conservatory.

I WAS SICK. SOME-ONE BROUGHT it to me in the HOSPITAL.

I NeeDeD SomeTHiNg to ReAD oN the PLANe. WHAT CAN I SAY? if WAS eiTHeR HeR OR LeO BuScAGLiA.

SHiRLey MAcLAiNe, WASN'T SHe iN — IRMA LA DOuce?

WHY SHOULD I tell YOU MY RESOLUTIONS? WHAT MAKES YOU tHINK I MADE ANY? DO YOU tHINK I SHOULD? IS tHAt it? YOU tHINK I SHOULD DO SOMETHING ABOUT MY EATING HABITS? IS tHAt it? ARE YOU BEING CRITICAL AGAIN? PEOPLE WHO LIVE the WAY YOU DO CAN'T AFFORD to be CRITICAL. WHAT DO YOU MEAN, "WHAT DO I MEAN?"

INSULTING CAT RATIONAL-IZATIONS.

the Accusation

LOOK AT THIS! IT'S RUINED!

I did not ruin your boring sweater by making tiny snags all over the front. I made a FASHION STATEMENT.

HARRY, YOU KNOW the worst thing About MAKING A REALLY BIG MISTAKE?

EVERYONE FINDS OUT WHAT AN idiot you ARE?

You CAN'T TRASH Someone else WHO'S MADE the SAME Mistake...

Not with a clear conscience.

At Least NOT FOR A WHILE.

EVEN SUPER-HEROES CAN't PLEASE EVERYONE.

there's A WOMAN IN A CAPE OUTSIDE.

THAT'S ALL I NeeD.

I KNOW YOU'VE BeeN UNDER A LOT OF PRESSURE, SO I took the LIBERTY OF PAYING YOUR BiLLS AND BALANCING YOUR CHECKBOOK. I DeFROSTED YOUR REFRIG-ERATOR AND FIXED THAT ANNOYING PING IN YOUR CAR. I BOUGHT YOU THIS BOUQUET.

YOU WENt INto MY APARTMENT? YOU touched MY CHECK-BOOK?

tomorrow-DR. RUTH AND A WHOLE studio AUDIENCE WILL TALK About their FIRST SEXUAL EXPERIENCE. AND I'LL EVEN TELL YOU MINE... "Geraldo" tomorrow at 9:00.

DON't, I BeG OF YOU.

FAMOUS CATS.

88

WILLPOWER IS AN OVER-RATED VIRTUE.

WHAT HAVE YOU SAID RECENTLY THAT YOU NEVER THOUGHT YOU'D HEAR YOURSELF SAY?

☐1. "I MUST HAVE LIPOSUCTION NOW."

☐2.

WHAT'S THE "PRE-VALENTINE'S DAY DIET SPECIAL"?

A SCOOP OF CURRIED TUNA SALAD, SCOOP OF COTTAGE CHEESE, AND WHILE YOU'RE EATING...

I DON'T THINK I'M UP TO IT... GIVE ME THE B.L.T.

THE COOK COMES OUT AND TELLS YOU HOW ADORABLE YOU ARE.

Alien Love♥ Can a Woman from a large midwestern town, on a lake, find perfect love on a distant planet?
HONEY.
BABY--CAKES.

95

Work Avoidance Techniques

Respectable

Honey, are you going to take the dog out or what?

Could you take him? I'm trying to reread all of Jane Austen.

tacky

We've got to work on our taxes. We've had one extension already.

Right after "Dynasty," O.K.?

You're like a son to me.

the Devil "Loses It," Momentarily.

I'll give you my immortal soul in exchange for a really dependable car, one that never breaks down or rusts.

NO, I can't bear it! Where are the people with verve and imagination— whose decadent requests tax my ingenuity?! Who wants your puny, boring, tiny soul, anyway?

Are you through?

Sedan or station wagon?

Lives of Susan

COMEDY MINI-SERIES ABOUT A WOMAN WITH A 3-WAY SPLIT PERSONALITY: HOUSEWIFE, ELECTRICIAN AND COMPULSIVE SHOPPER.

SUSAN is CLEANING HER CLOSET AND SLAPPING the side of HER heAd every time she comes ACROSS AN outFit she Loved in the store AND HAtED AS soon As she got it home, when she ACCIDENtALLy KNocks HerseLF out. SHe comes to At A SHoe Boutique WHiLe trying ON A PAIR OF WHite SATIN PUMPS WitH SPike HEeLS.

the Devil chats about haircuts in Hell
In Hell when you get a bad haircut it never grows out.

103

Lingerie Lady ("SOMEONE to CARE...About YOUR underwear")

I don't want to EMBARRASS you, but I KNOW tHAt YOUR underwear's IN tAtteRS, so I took the Liberty OF PURCHASING A Selection OF ELEGANt Lingerie FOR YOU. I put it AWAY AND ALSO StRAIGHtened YOUR dRAWERS.

WHO ARE YOU? YOU WHАt? THANKS!

Hi, this is Patty Murphy... Cher called a news conference today to announce that she wouldn't be exercising any more.

"I know I'm a role model for women, so I figure if I let myself go a little, they can relax," said a repentant Cher.

a the Sylvia School of Scientific Writing

Bonus Word: HOT FLASH

Students please use the bonus word one more time in the paragraph below:

"I'm experiencing a hot flash," said Esmeralda throwing off her cape, and various other articles of clothing. _____

Pick the correct definition of HOT FLASH below:

☐1. An explosion caused by careless use of matches.

☐2. A brilliant idea you get in the middle of the night, but forget by morning.

the Sylvia School of Languages

OUR MOTTO "WHY LEARN MORE than you NEED?"

I WANT to LEARN to SAY: "CALL this A SOFT-boiled eGG? SURELY YOU Jest."

LEARN the PHRASES MOST USEFUL WHEN TRAVELING OUTSIDE the COUNTRY—IN 5 LANGUAGES.
1. "I AM NOT PERSONALLY RESPONSIBLE FOR MY GOVERNMENT'S FOREIGN POLICY."
2. "TAKE ME to the REAL AIRPORT."

yes, we ARE ALL NATIVE speakers.

SO WHO'S GOING to WIN the PRESIDENTIAL ELECTION?

Don't you WANT to KNOW if there's A SUMMER ROMANCE IN YOUR FUTURE?

NO, REALLY I COULDN'T CARE LESS. I WAS IN the NEIGH-BORHOOD, I THOUGHT I WOULD JUST DROP BY.

I SEE A MAN SO ADORABLE THAT WOMEN ARE FALL-ING ALL OVER HIM, but HE'S LOOK-ING AT YOU.

At ME?

ACTUALLY, A LITTLE to YOUR LEFT.

109

How big is your Ego?

I don't HAVE AN ego. I'M Just A simple country LAWYER.

GiGANtic! ANy other guy would SNAP from the STRAin of carrying it Around.

I DreAMt the doctor removed MY ego, AND it WAS SMALLer than everyone else's. I HEARD SNickers.

I WAS GOING to SPEND the AFTERNOON QUIETLY READING AND

DRYING SOME LINGERIE IN the MICROWAVE.

HARRY, DON'T YOU THINK PAT SAJAK IS PATRONIZING TO VANNA WHITE? LIKE AT THE BEGINNING OF THE SHOW WHEN SHE COMES OUT AND SHOWS OFF Her dress AND HE SAYS SOMETHING Like, "VANNA CAN WALK BETTER THAN ANYBODY." LIKE it's A MIRACLE SHE CAN WALK AND SMILE?

I CAN'T BELIEVE I SAID THAT.

I DON'T EVEN WATCH "WHEEL OF FORTUNE."

I think YOU'RE CHANNELING.

VOLUME START

OFF   ON

the SYLVIA SCHOOL OF WRITING BONUS WORD: Conflagration

LYdiA Looked FOR MORE LOGS to Put oN the FIRE, but there weren't ANY. So SHE turned to the bookshelf AND PULLED down: SMART WOMEN, FOOLISH CHOICES; MEN WHO HATE WOMEN AND the WOMEN WHO LOVE them; HOW to LOVE A DIFFICULT MAN; WOMEN WHO LOVE too MUCH, AND MEN WHO CAN'T LOVE, AND THREW them oN the FIRE. "WHAT A LOVELY CONFLAGRATION they MAKE," SHE murmured HAPPILY to HERSELF.

DID YOU HAVE A ROTTEN MOTHER WHO WASN'T FAMOUS? Do you COMPLAIN to YOUR FRIENDS: "Other PEOPLE WHO HAD LOUSY CHILDHOODS At LEAST GOT A BOOK OUT OF IT." WELL NOW YOU CAN, too! the SYLVIA SMALL PRESS WILL GHOSTWRITE AND PUBLISH YOUR CHILDHOOD. CALL 1-800-I'LL-PAY. BAD FATHERS ½ PRICE.

Hi, MOM. YOU'RE At the GROCERY? YOU DOUBLE PARKED AND RAN IN to GET A QUART OF MILK?

YOU LEFT the ENGINE RUNNING, AND NOW YOU REALIZE YOU LOCKED the KEYS IN the CAR?

Do I HAVE AN EXTRA SET OF KEYS?

MOM, I LIVE IN CLEVE-LAND.

Anxiety checklist for the Morning

OMIGOD, it's Another DAY!

☐1. WILL REAGAN'S NEXT SUPREME COURT NOMINEE be even worse?

☐2. DO I HAVE ANY CLEAN SOCKS?

☐3. WILL MY EYES EVER OPEN ANY WIDER?

Love Cop — RAcing HITHER AND YON to keep incompatible couples from getting together — CAN relax in the winter, because no one leaves their Apartment.

OH sure, maybe it slows down on the east coast, but there's still California, where they Never stop.

You're thrilled that GARY HART's back in the RACE, AND yet You're so adorable I can't keep MY HANDS OFF You

You refuse to Jog, AND you read too MUCH, but I tremble WHEN I'M NEAR YOU.

IF the EARTH MOVES under YOUR Feet, it's Probably A QUAKE. Get AWAY FROM EACH other before I become really irritated!

the Dogs from Hell

JUST TWO MISUNDER-STOOD PUPPIES.

Out of SHAPE? Need exercise, but LACK Motivation? INQUIRE WITHIN.

Hi.

WE'LL HAVE YOUR PULSE RATE UP IN NO time.

THE AIRLINES ARE CRACKING DOWN. THEY'RE ONLY ALLOWING 2 PIECES OF CARRY-ON LUGGAGE — PER PERSON. I guess SOME PEOPLE TOOK ADVANTAGE OF THEM.

SOME OF THOSE PEOPLE ARE HERE RIGHT NOW.

REMEMBER the time I RUSHED ONTO the PLANE JUST AS the door WAS CLOSING, WITH that RUBBER RAFT AND INSISTED it WOULD FIT IN the OVER-HEAD COMPARTMENT?

perfectly-